Let's Color
Cactus and Succulents

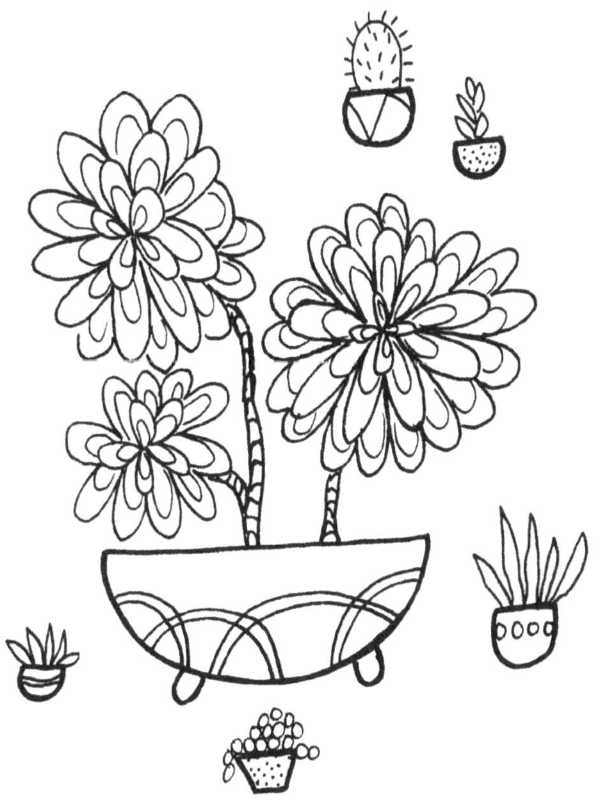

Featuring the art of Cara Gregor

ISBN 978-1-7329722-1-6

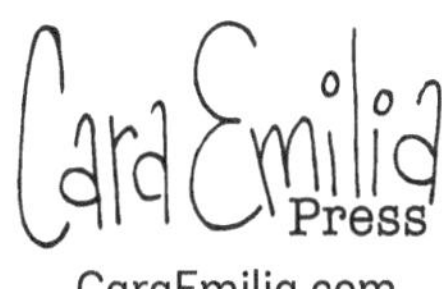

CaraEmilia.com

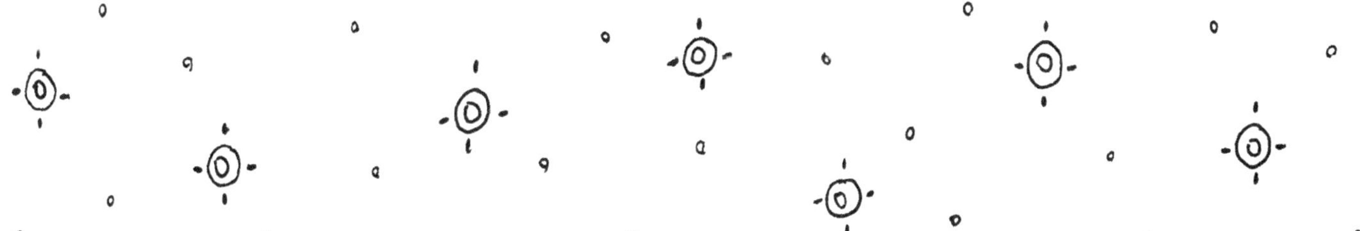

Hi, I'm Cara Gregor, the illustrator of *Let's Color: Cactus and Succulents*. I am a painter, illustrator, and creative living in Sacramento, CA, and as you can guess... I am **OBSESSED** with succulents! They are just such amazing plants with amazing colors and shapes. Sometimes they seem like they are from ancient times, underwater, or from another planet and they are incredibly resilient. For this book I thought it would be fun to share some life lessons that I have learned from these inspirational plants.

Lesson 1: Be the beautiful YOU that YOU are

Succulents and cactus are so different from other plants with their water filled interiors. Their differences don't bother them however, and they just grow as beautiful as they can wherever they are. Even if all the flowers and trees are different, they turn their faces to the sun and say "I'm growing too and I am beautiful!"

Lesson 2: Love what you have

Many plants like to have their space, but succulents and cacti flourish when they are close to each other. They don't need much to be happy and love to grow in groups. They beg the question, "How can we flourish with what we have and the people in our life?"

Lesson 3: Explore and make lemonade

When a succulent petal or piece of cactus gets broken or cut off the broken piece can grow roots and build a new home in almost any favorable environment. They are not afraid to explore and happily build a new home wherever they can, making lemonade from lemons.

Basically I think I am so attracted to succulents and cactus because they are happy plants that don't need much. A "happy go lucky" attitude can go a long way in life and brings many unforeseen adventures and wonderful people into the mix. Enjoy coloring these beautiful happy plants. Think of their life lessons, relax, and be the beautiful you that you are!

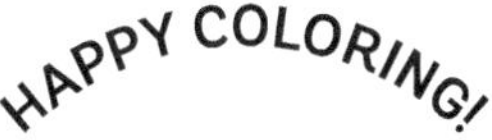

More of Cara Gregor's work can be found online at
CaraEmilia.com and on instagram @caraemiliadesigns.

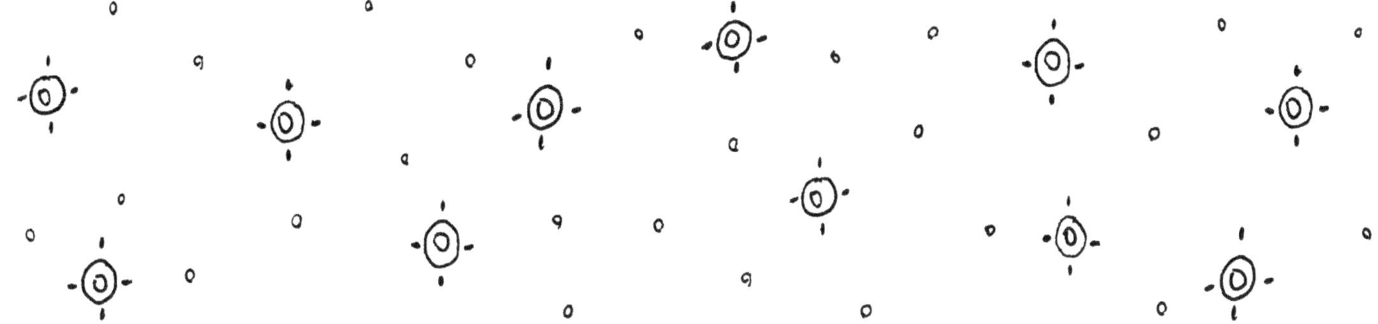

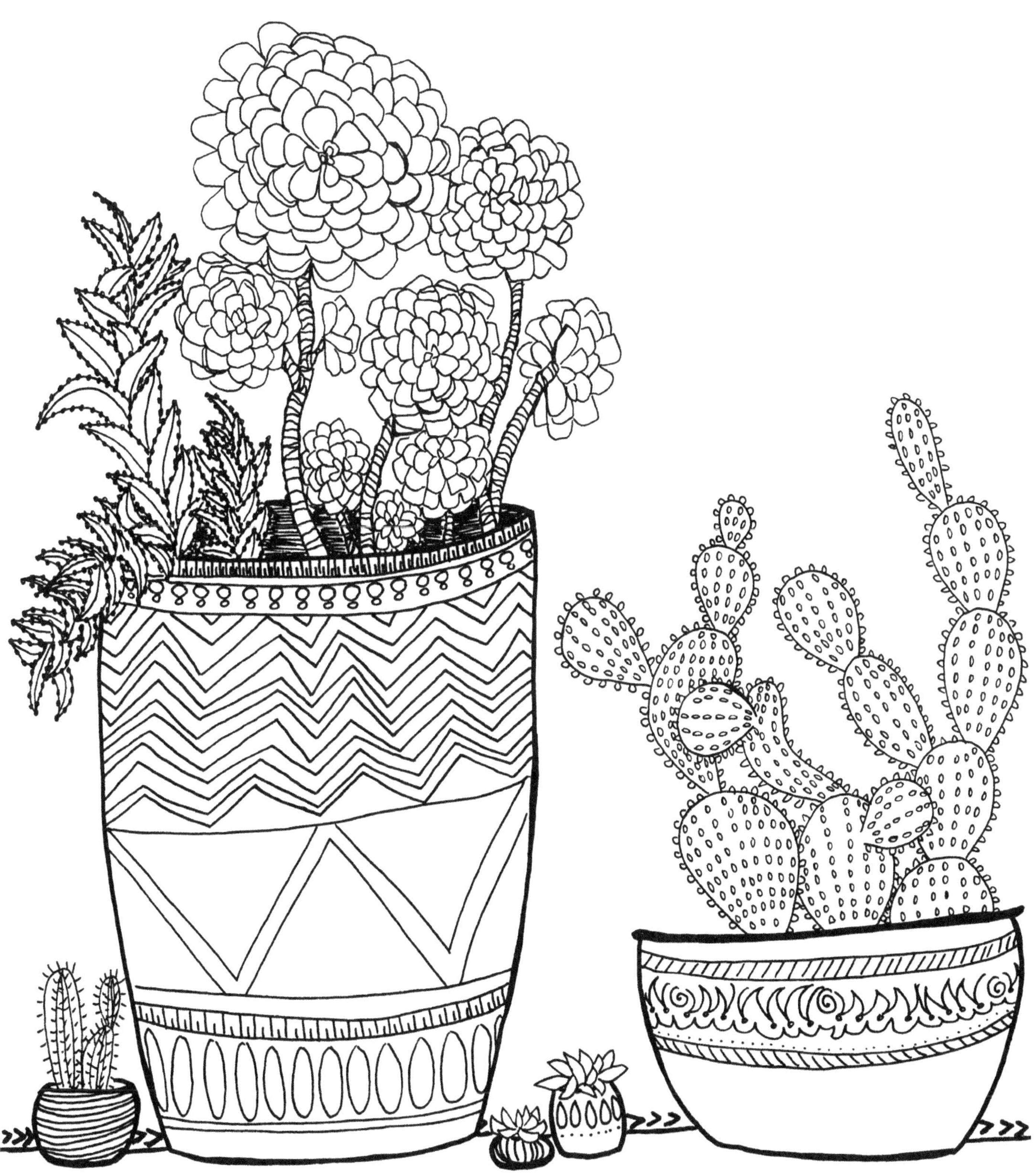

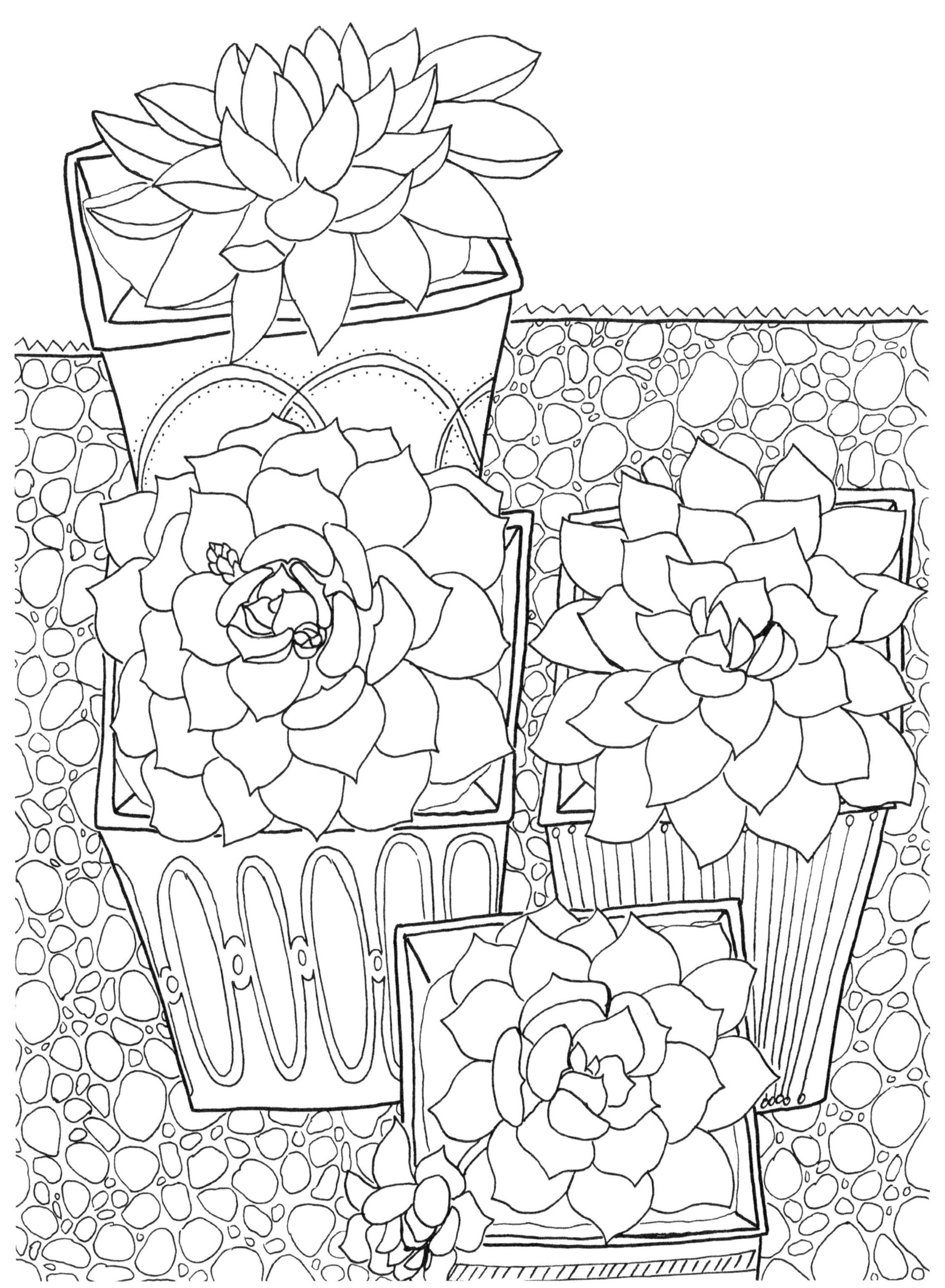

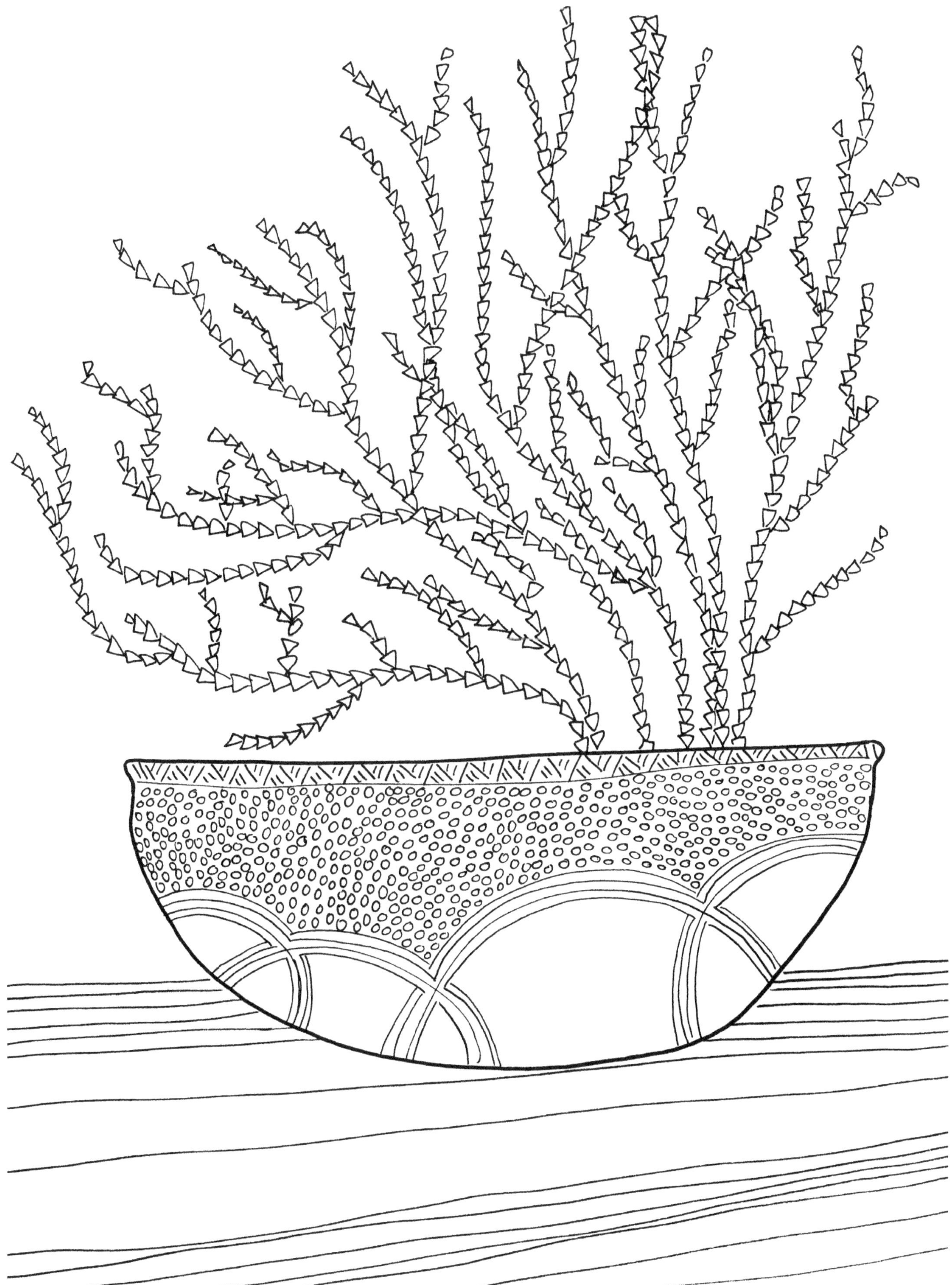

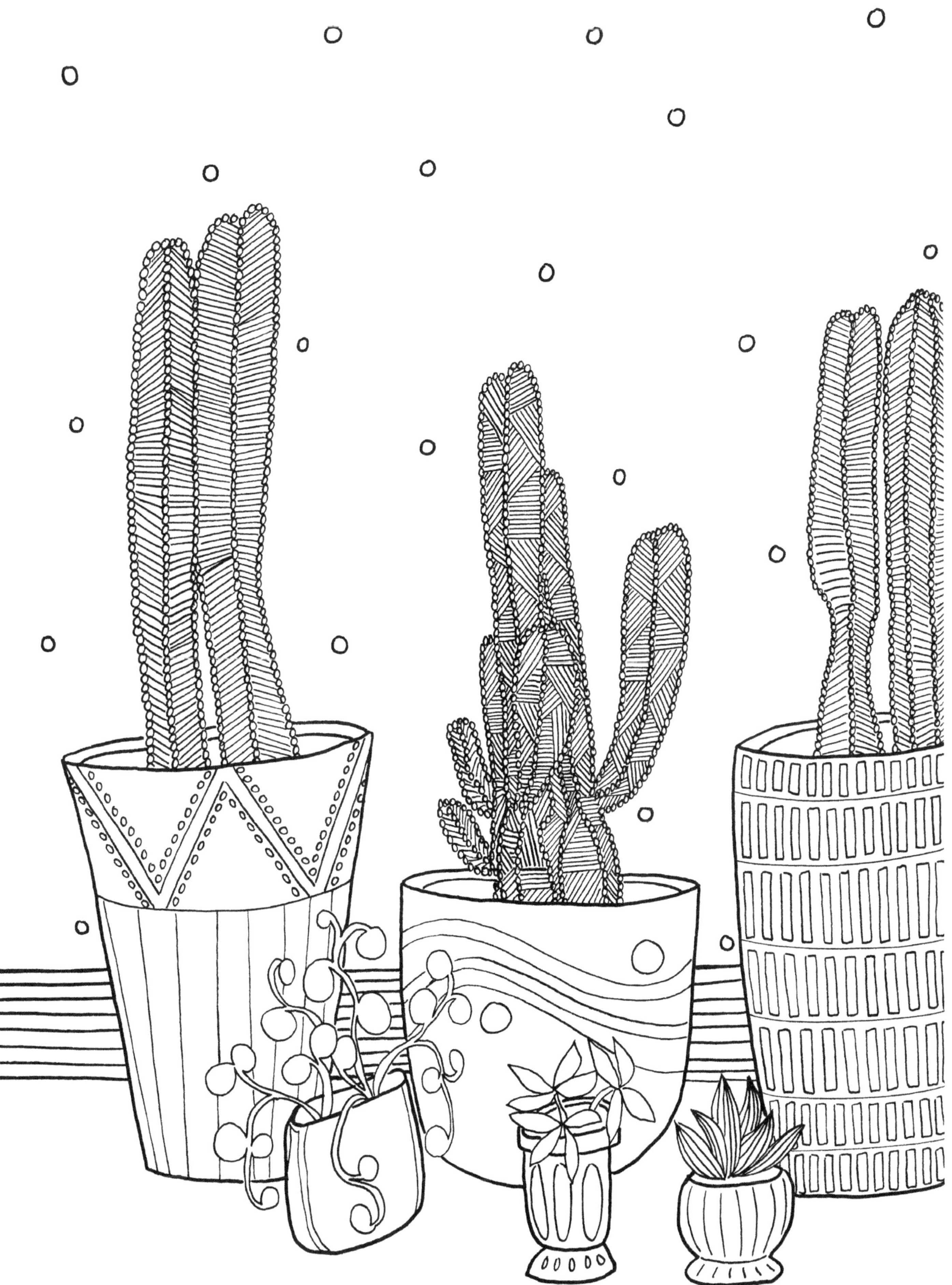

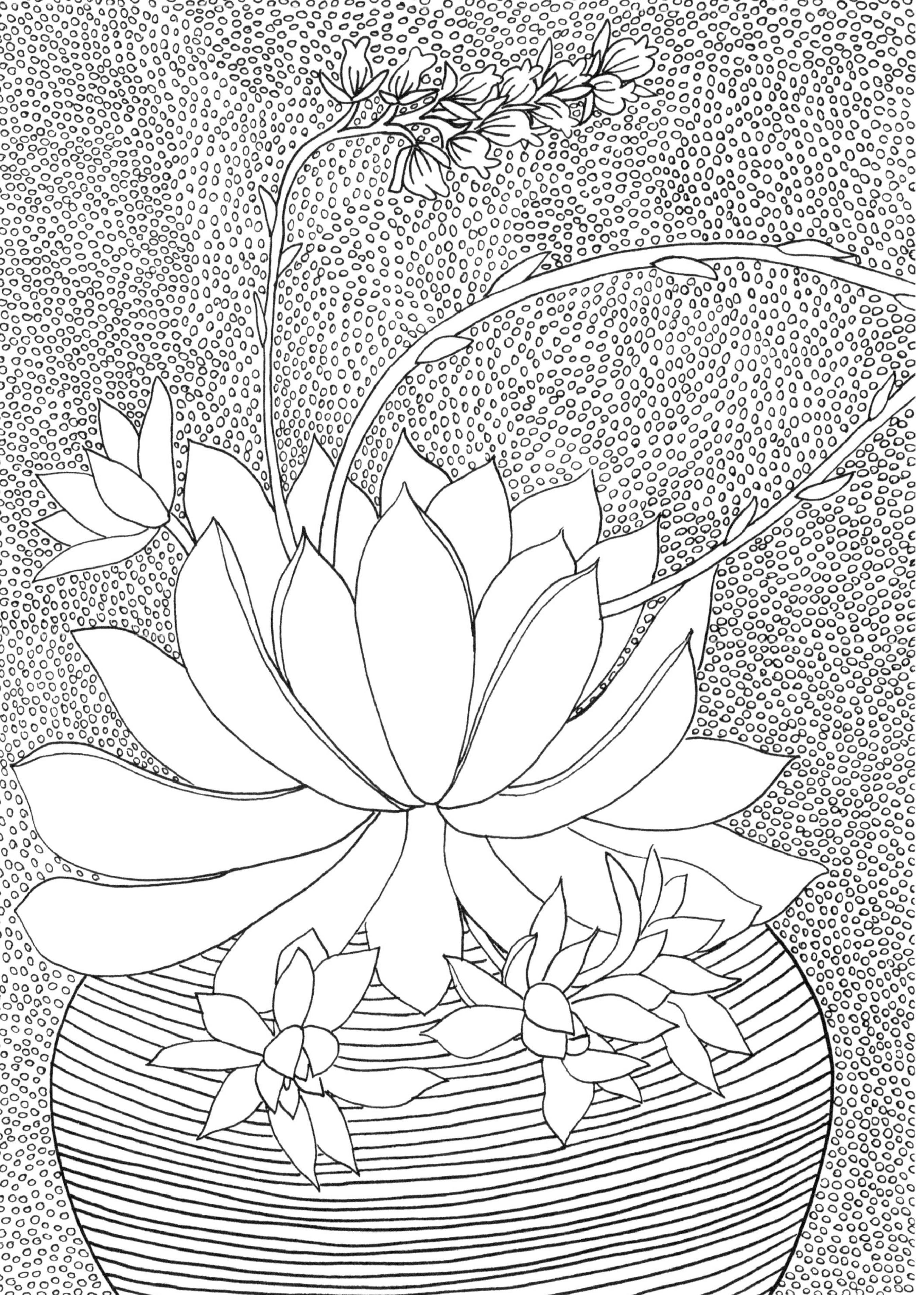

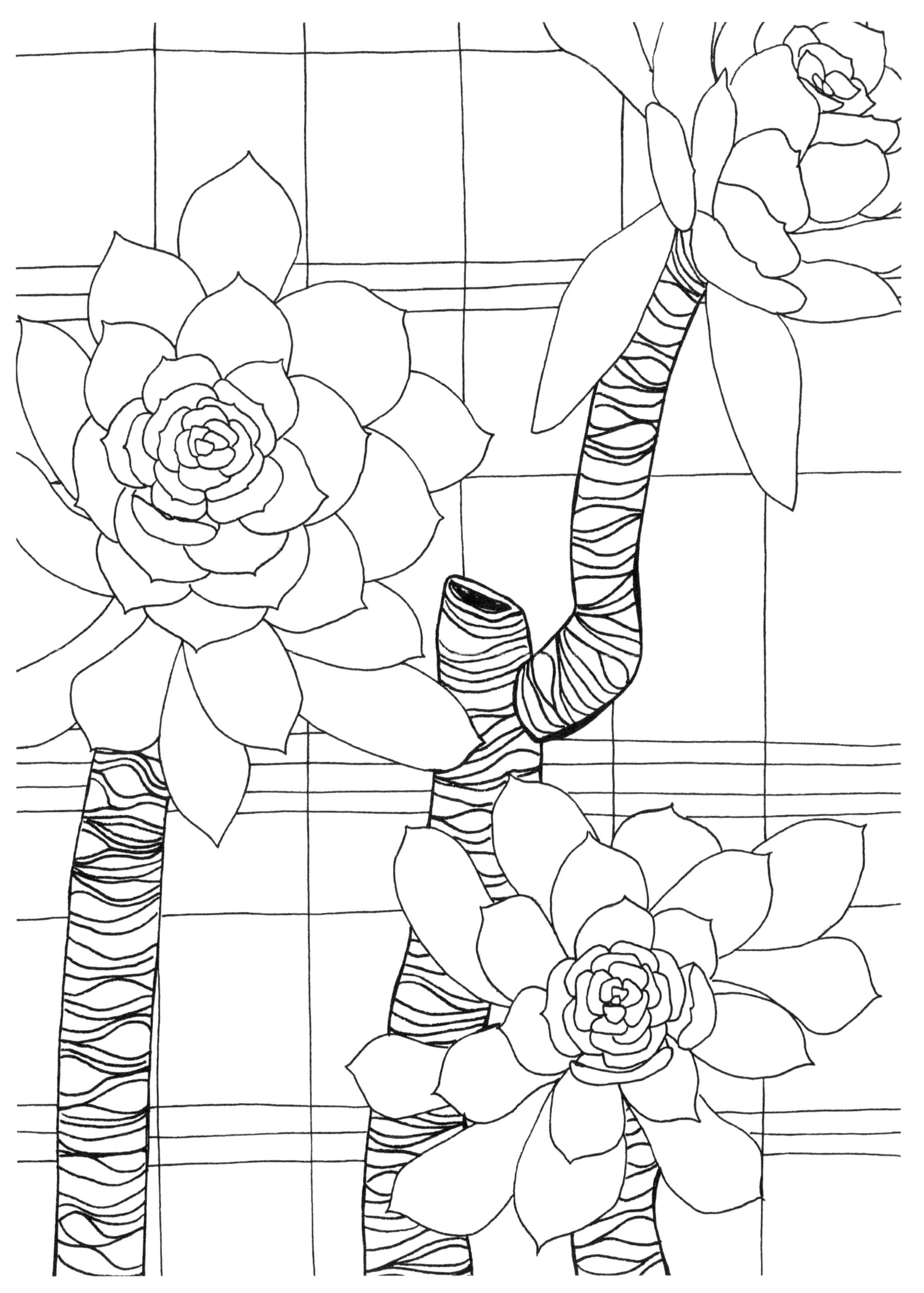

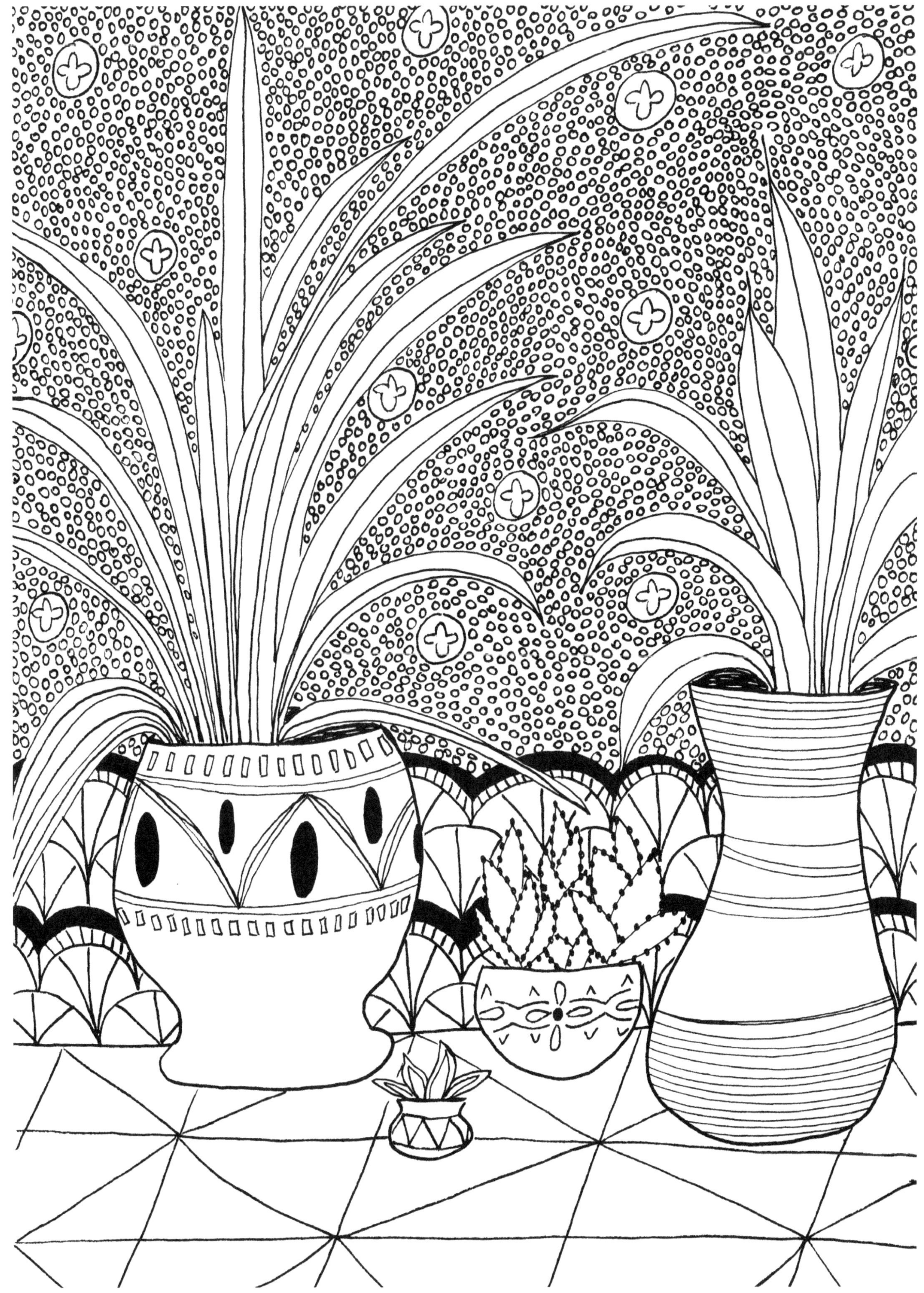

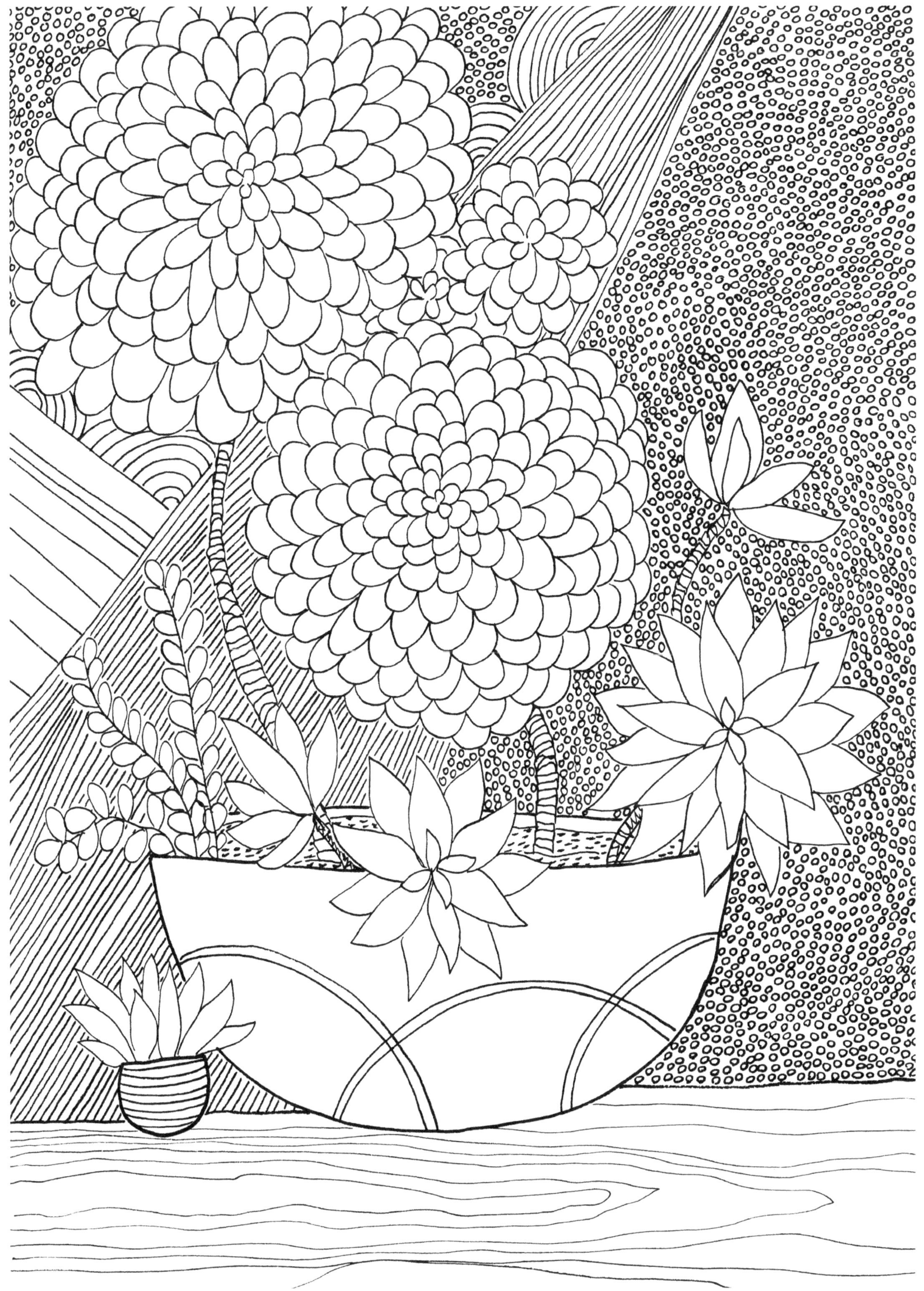

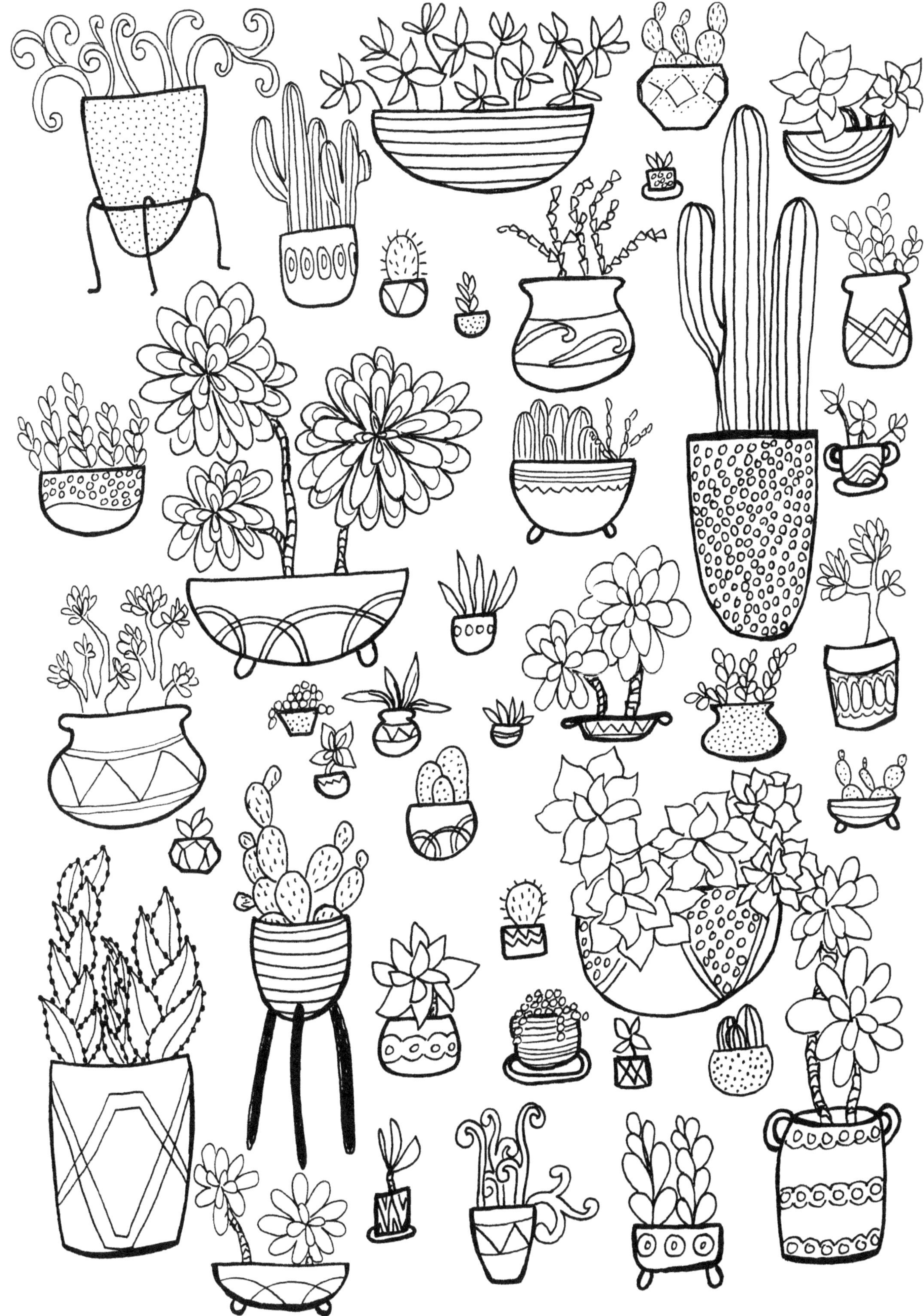

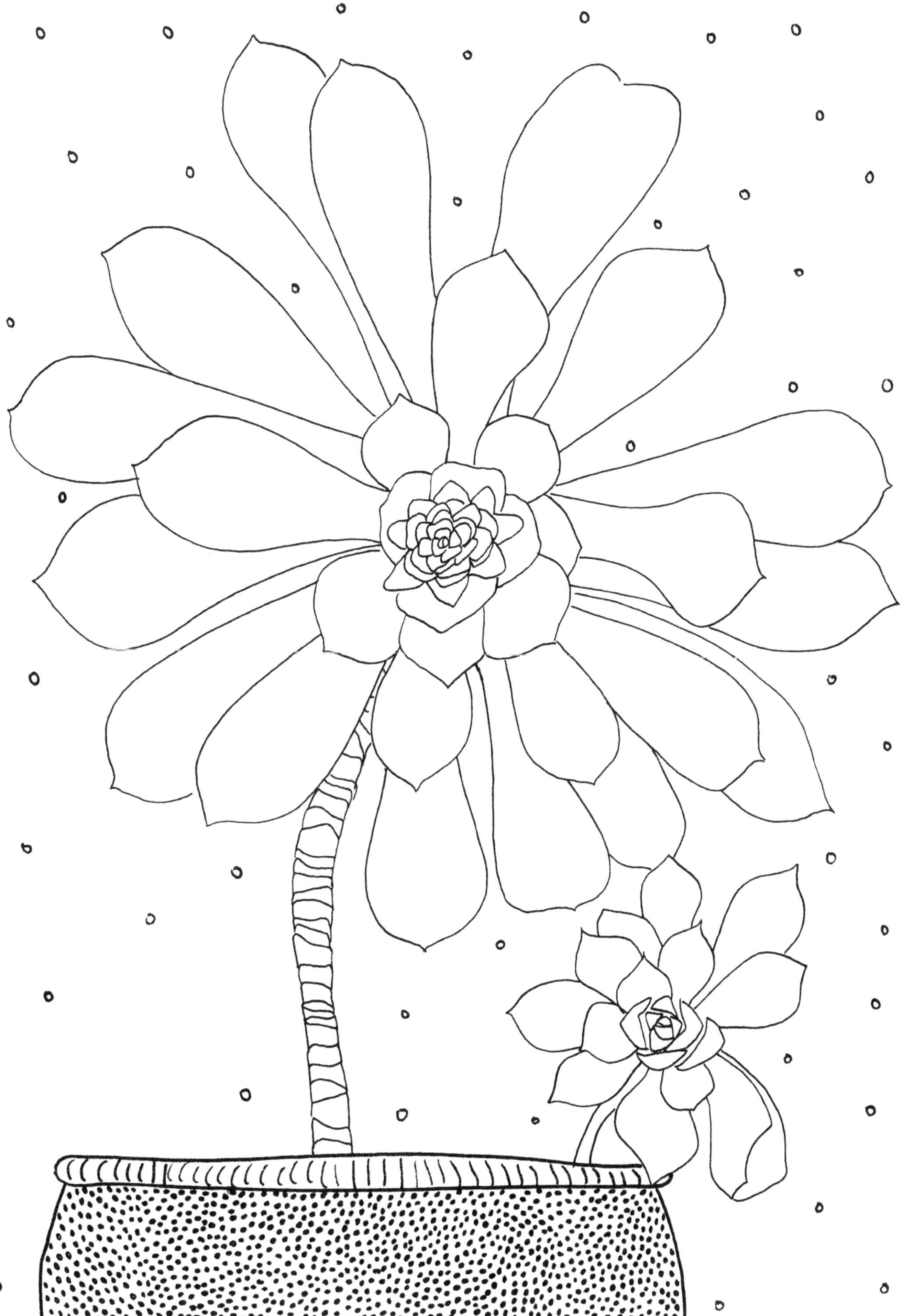

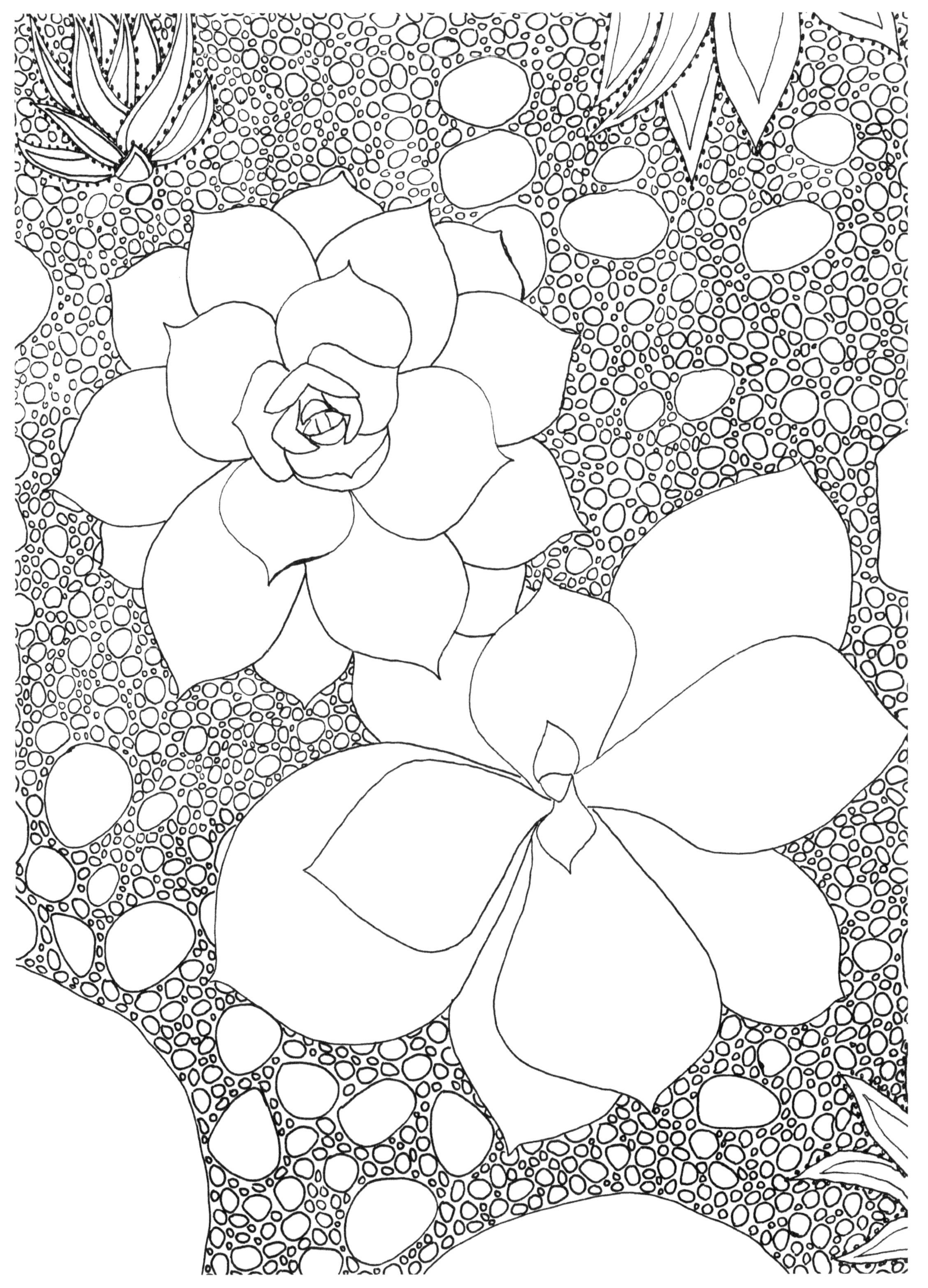

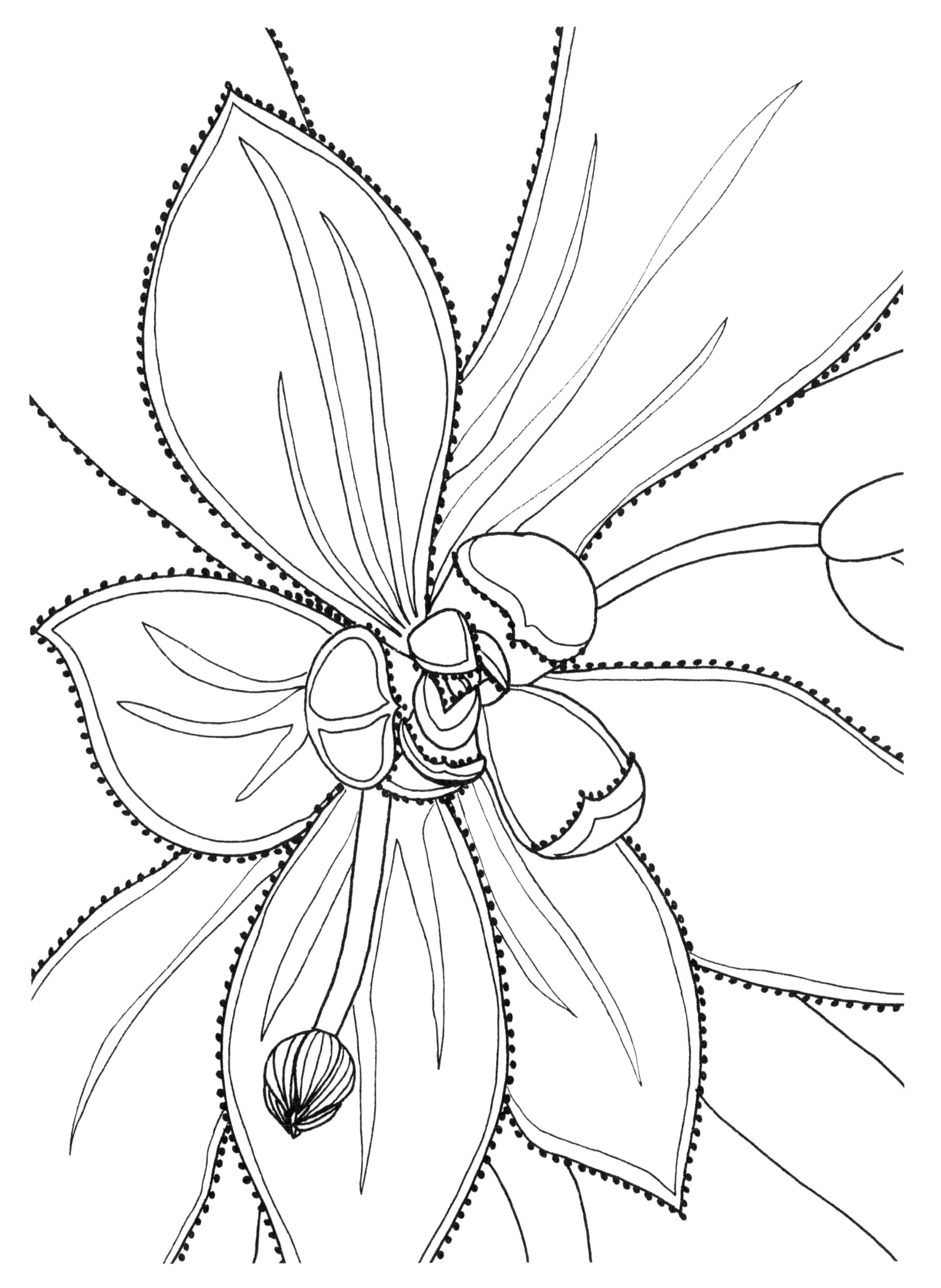

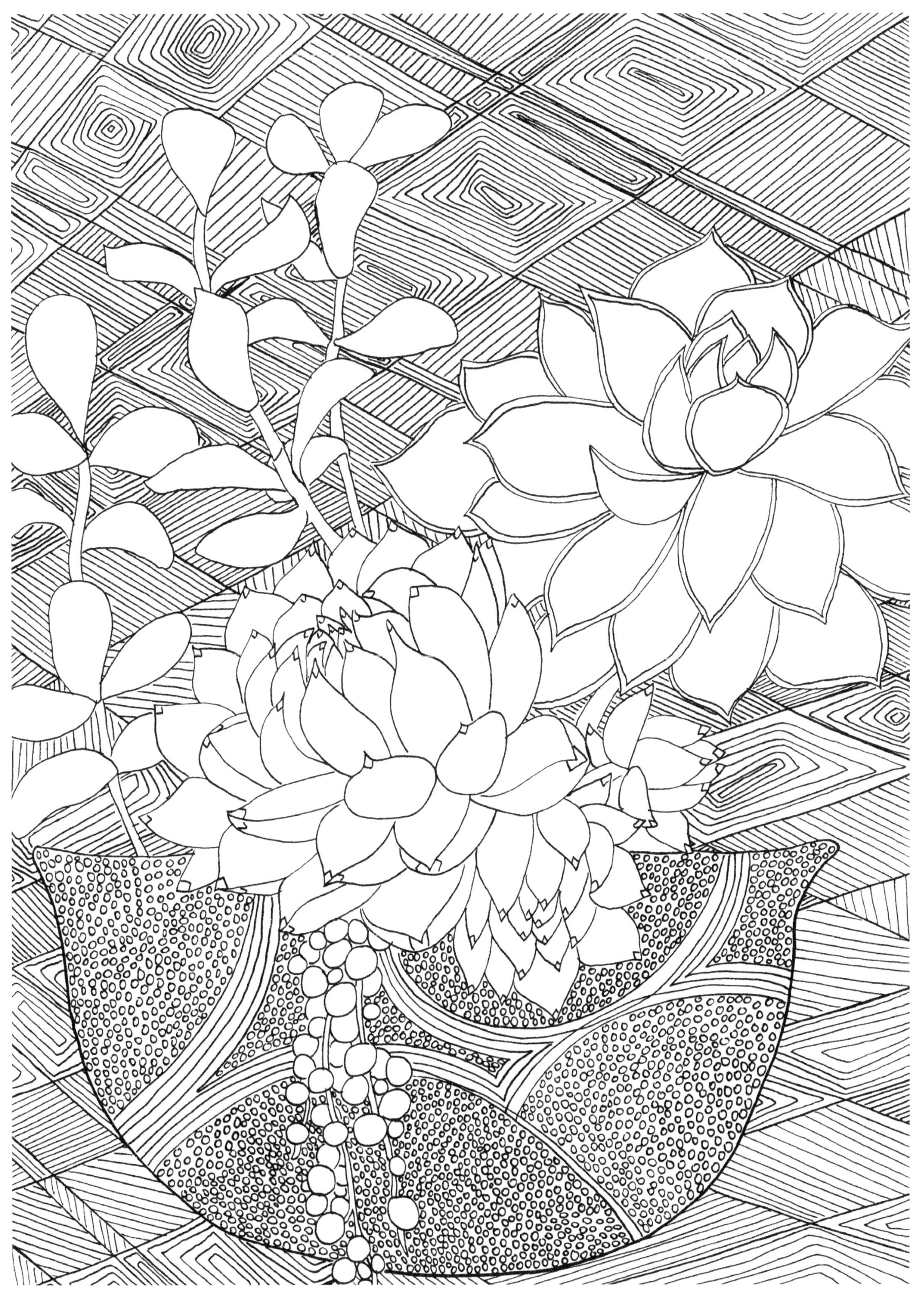

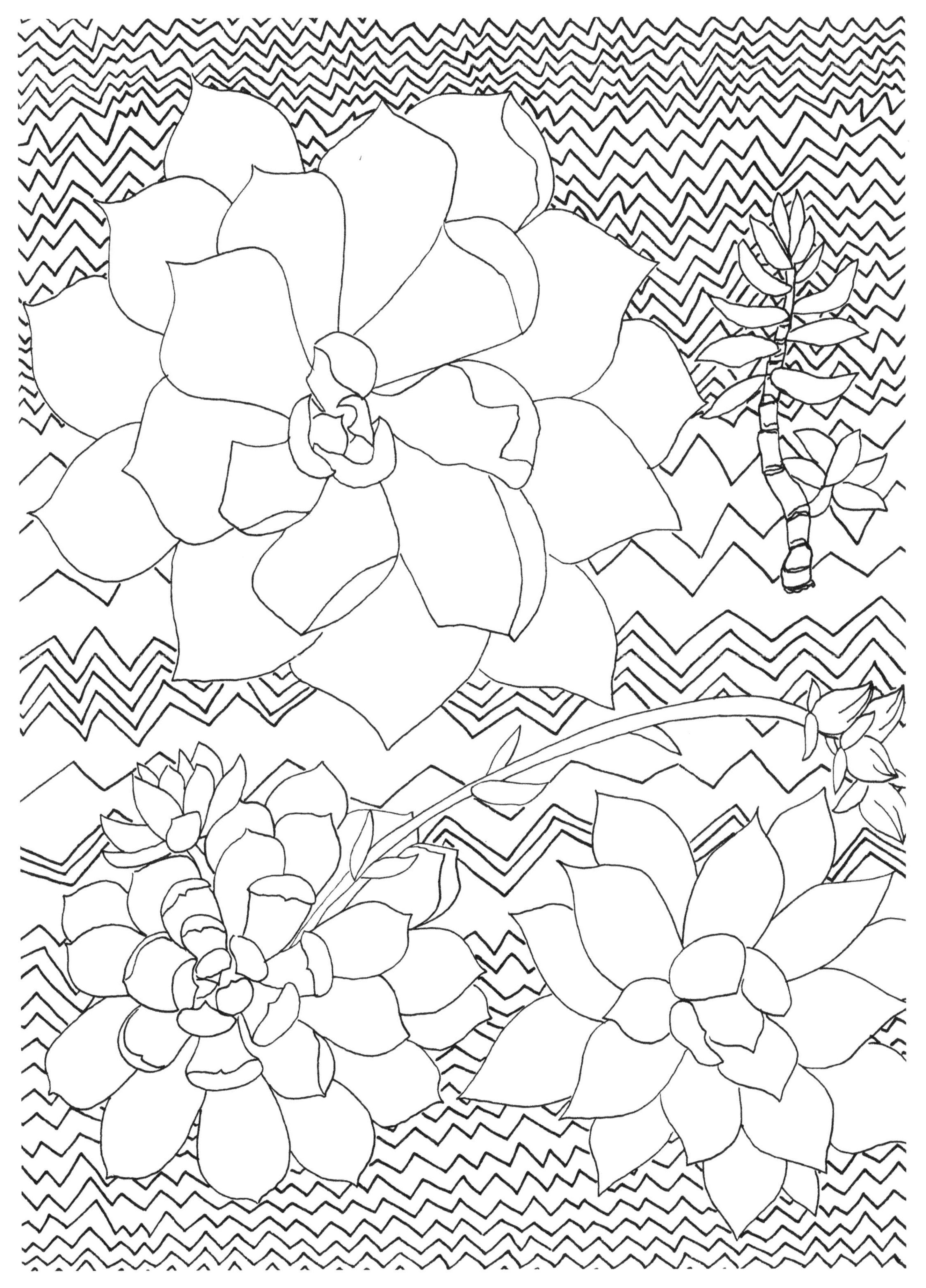

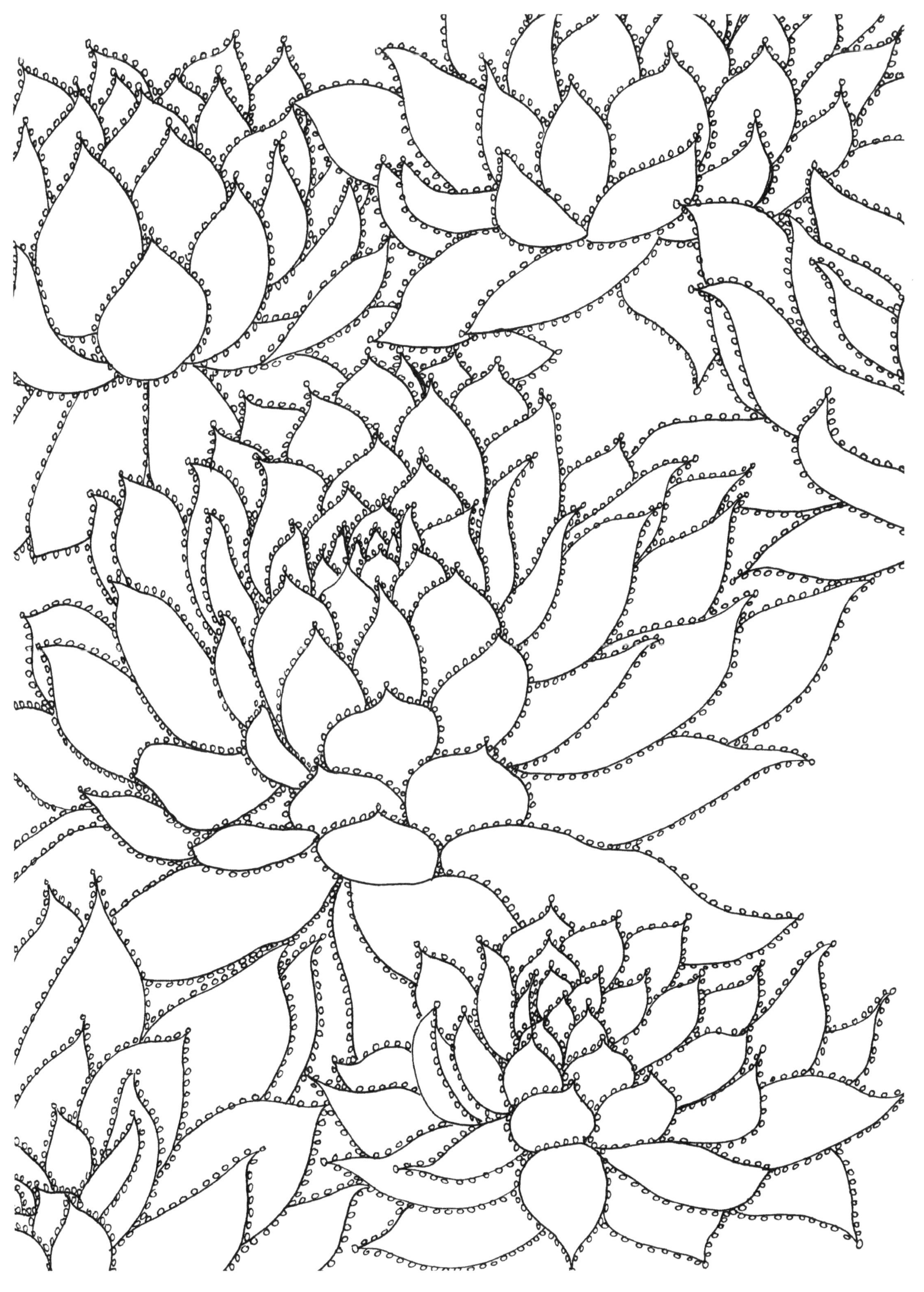

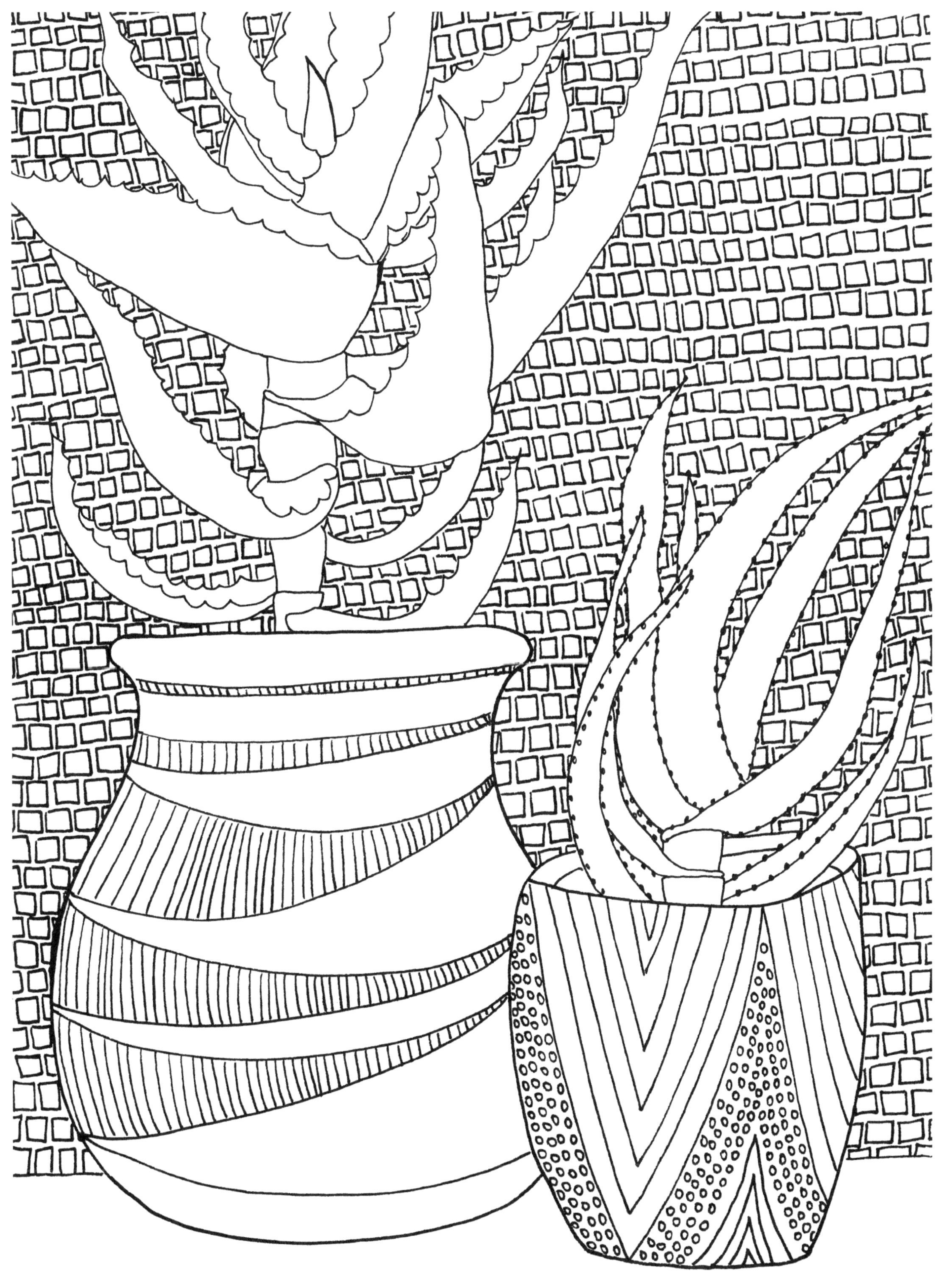

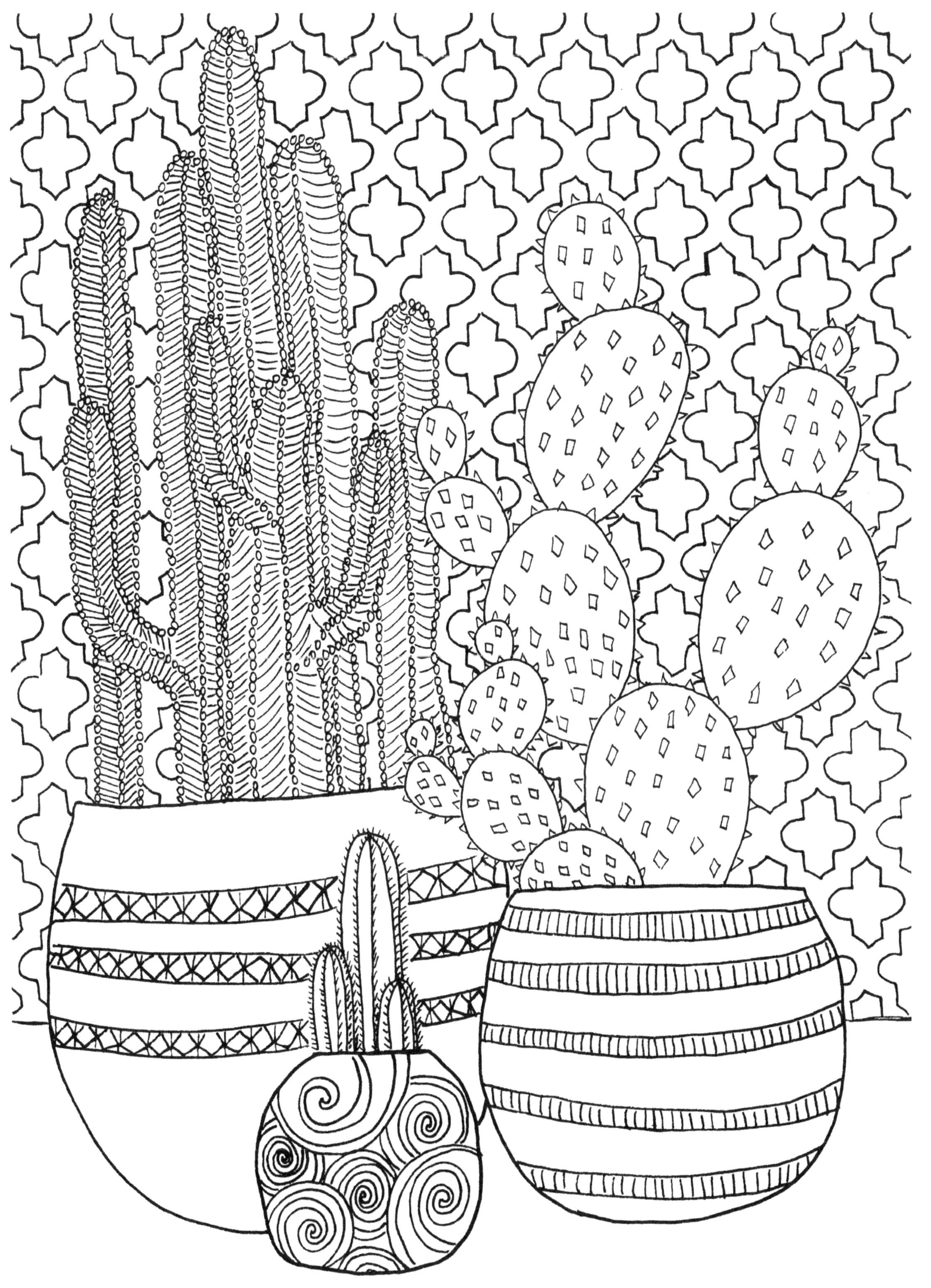

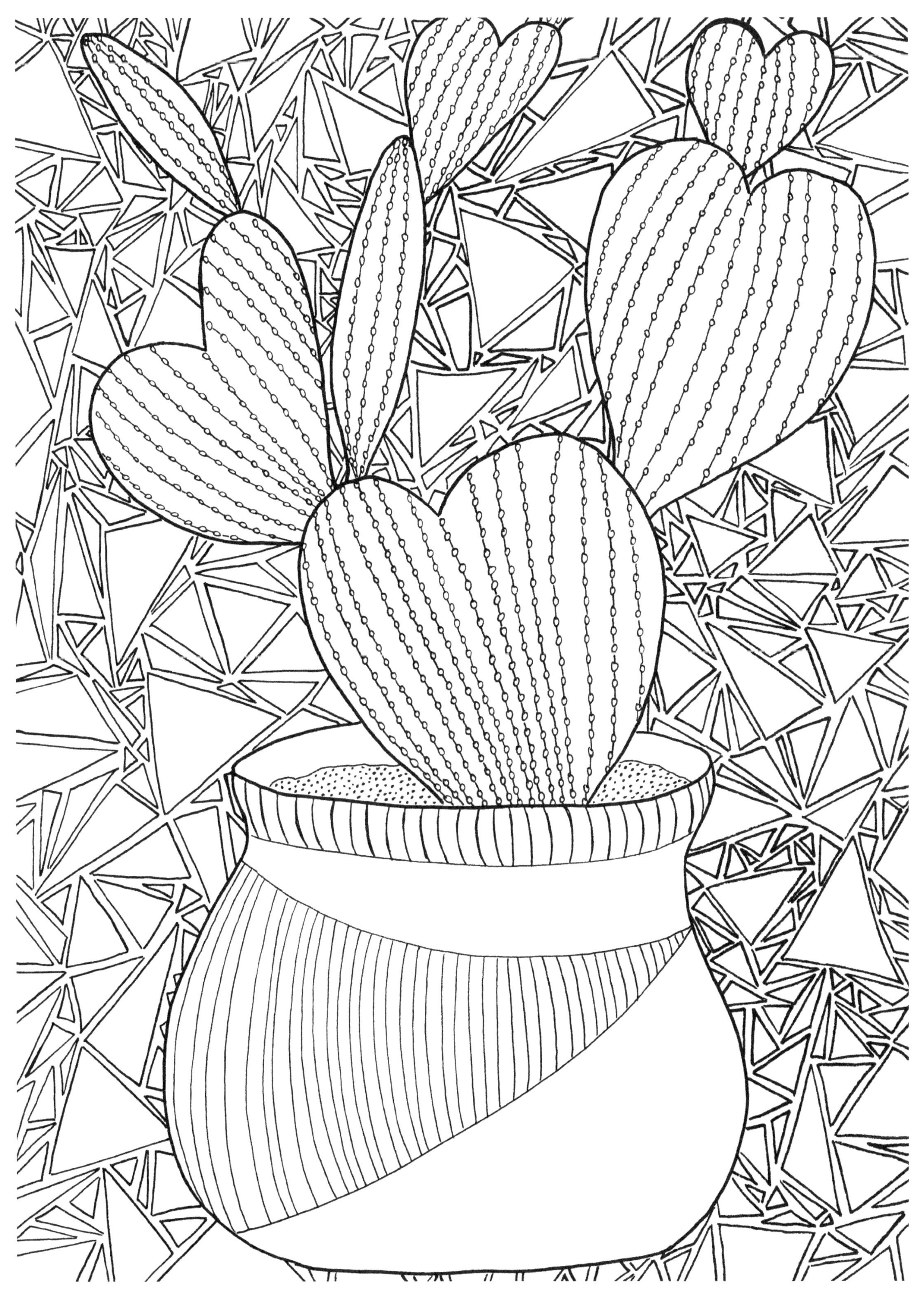

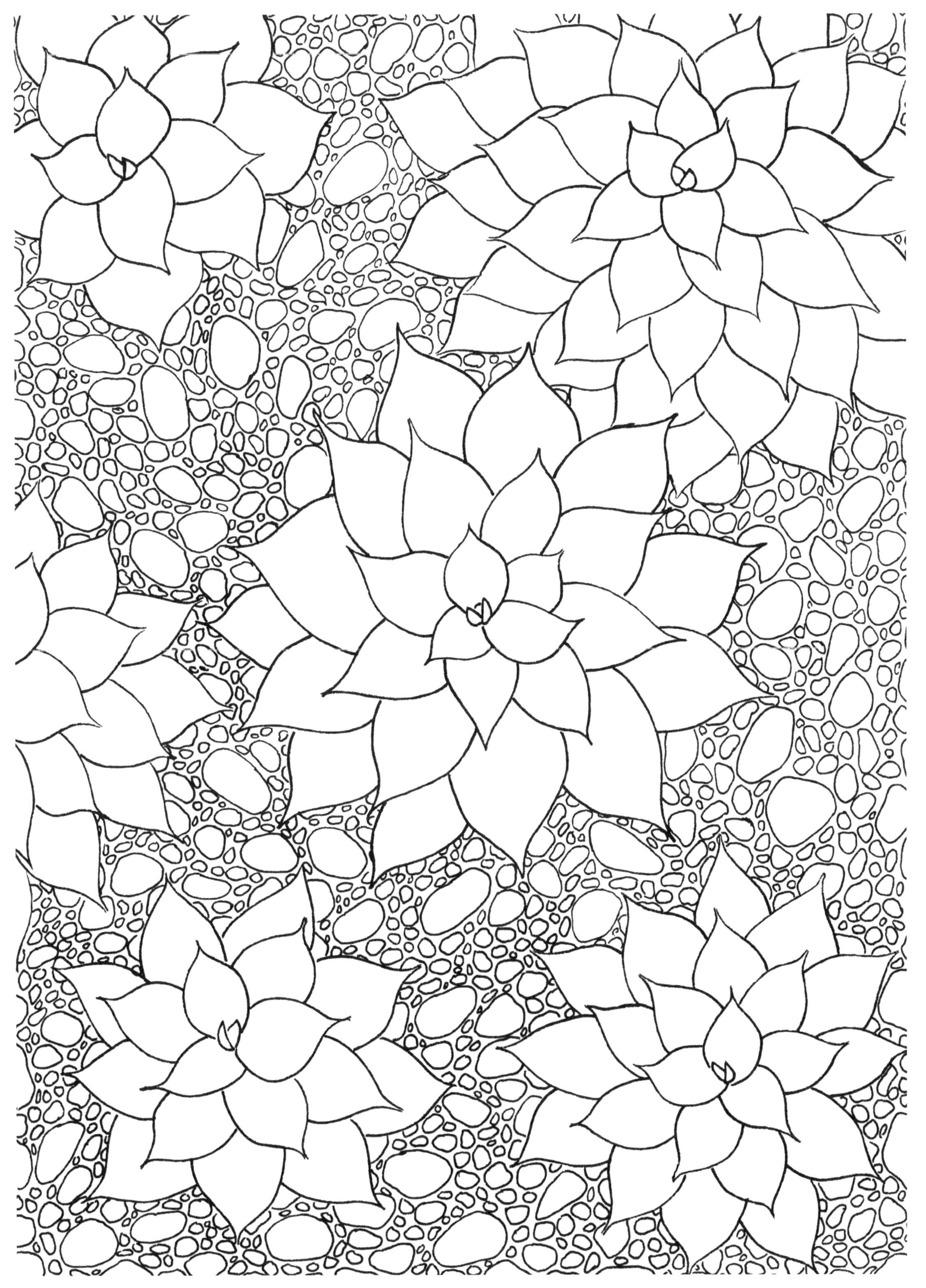

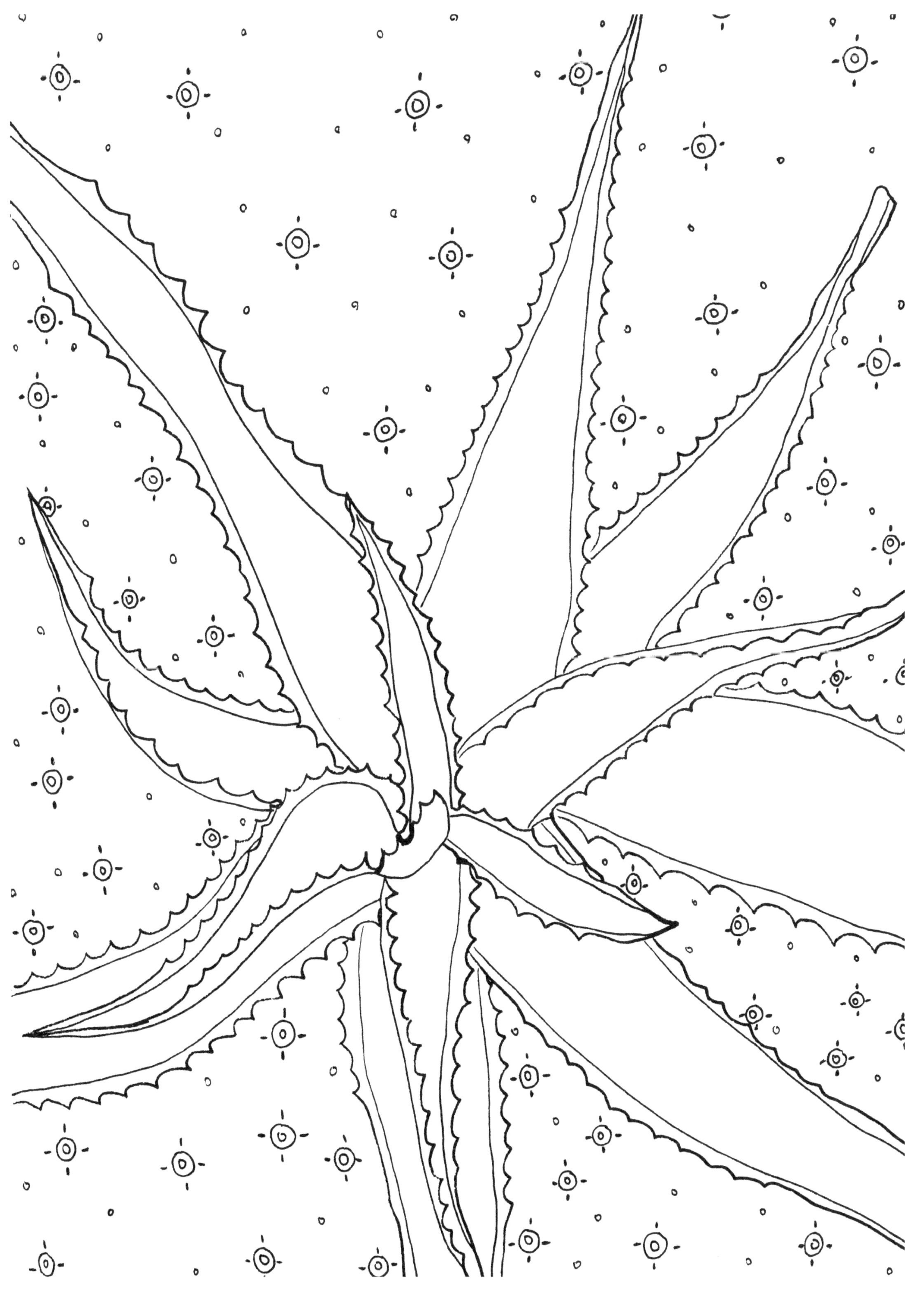

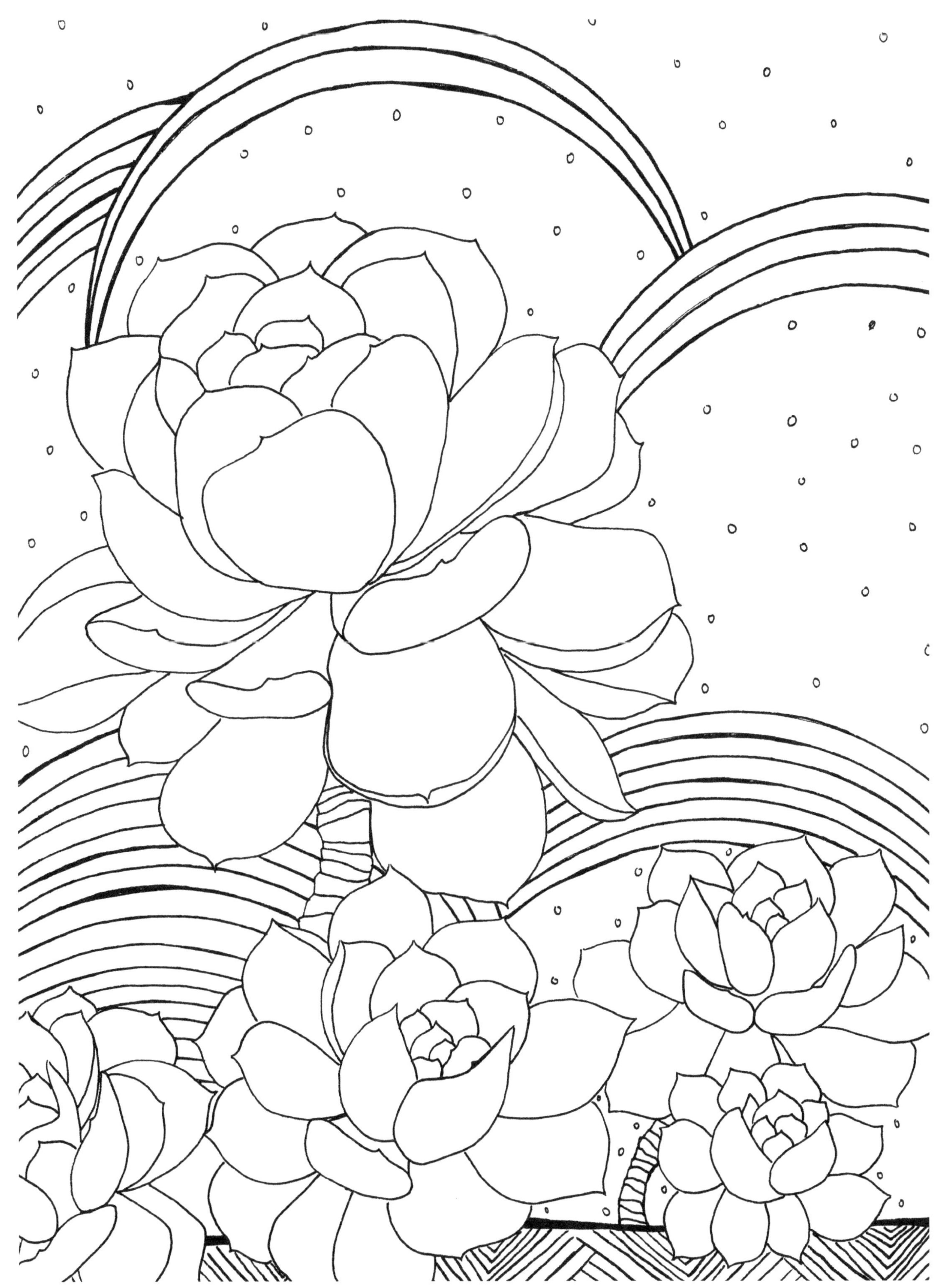

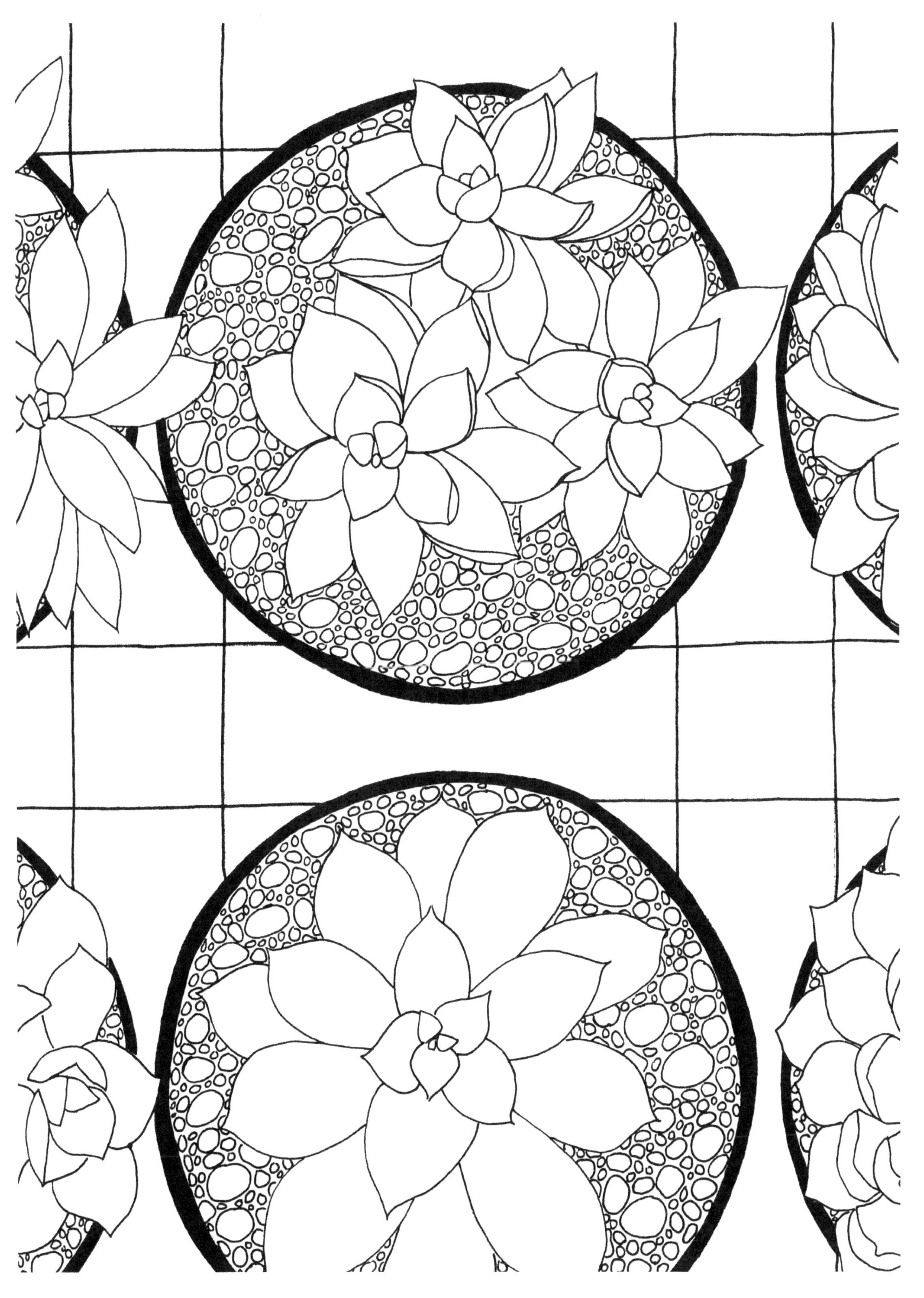

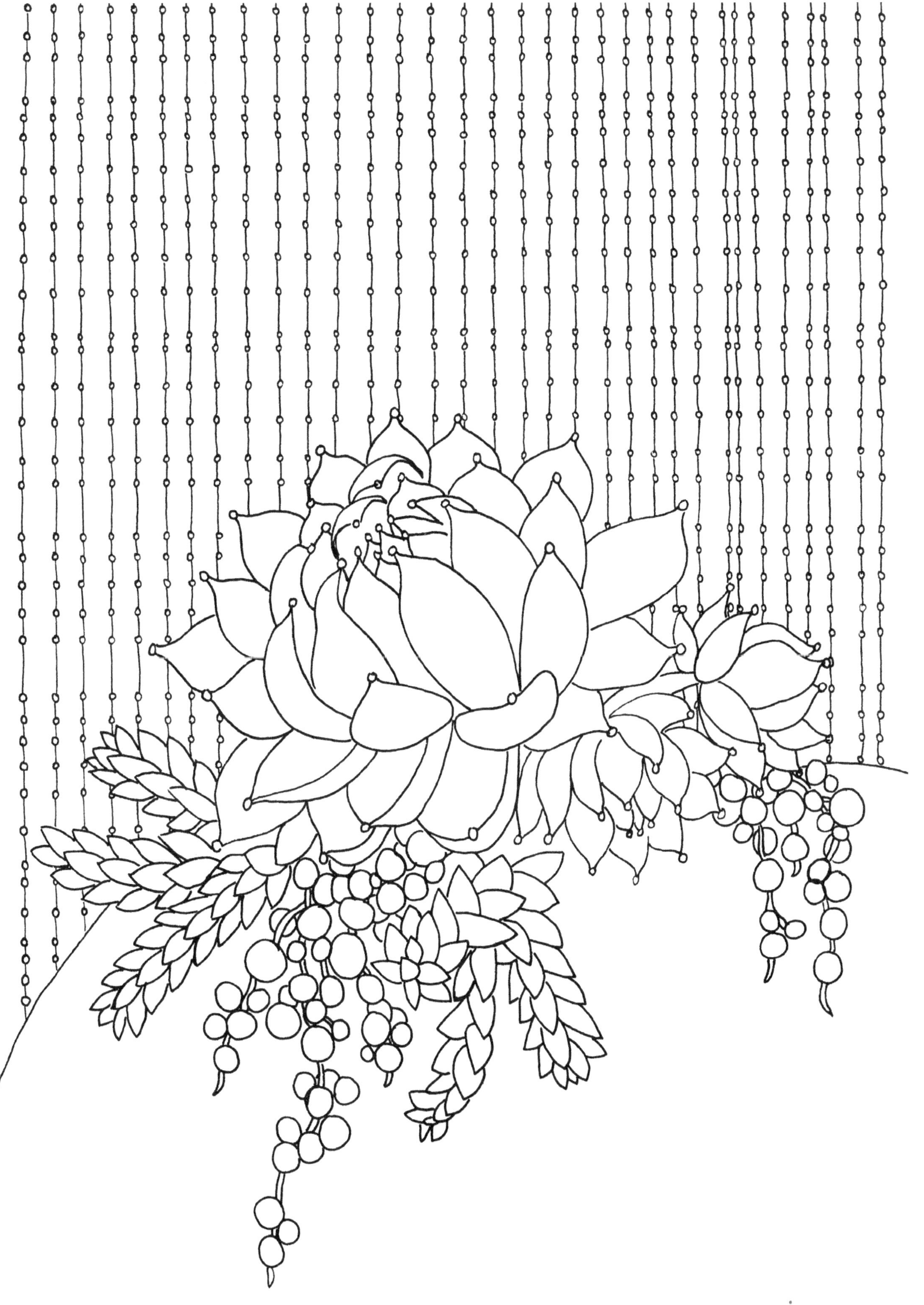

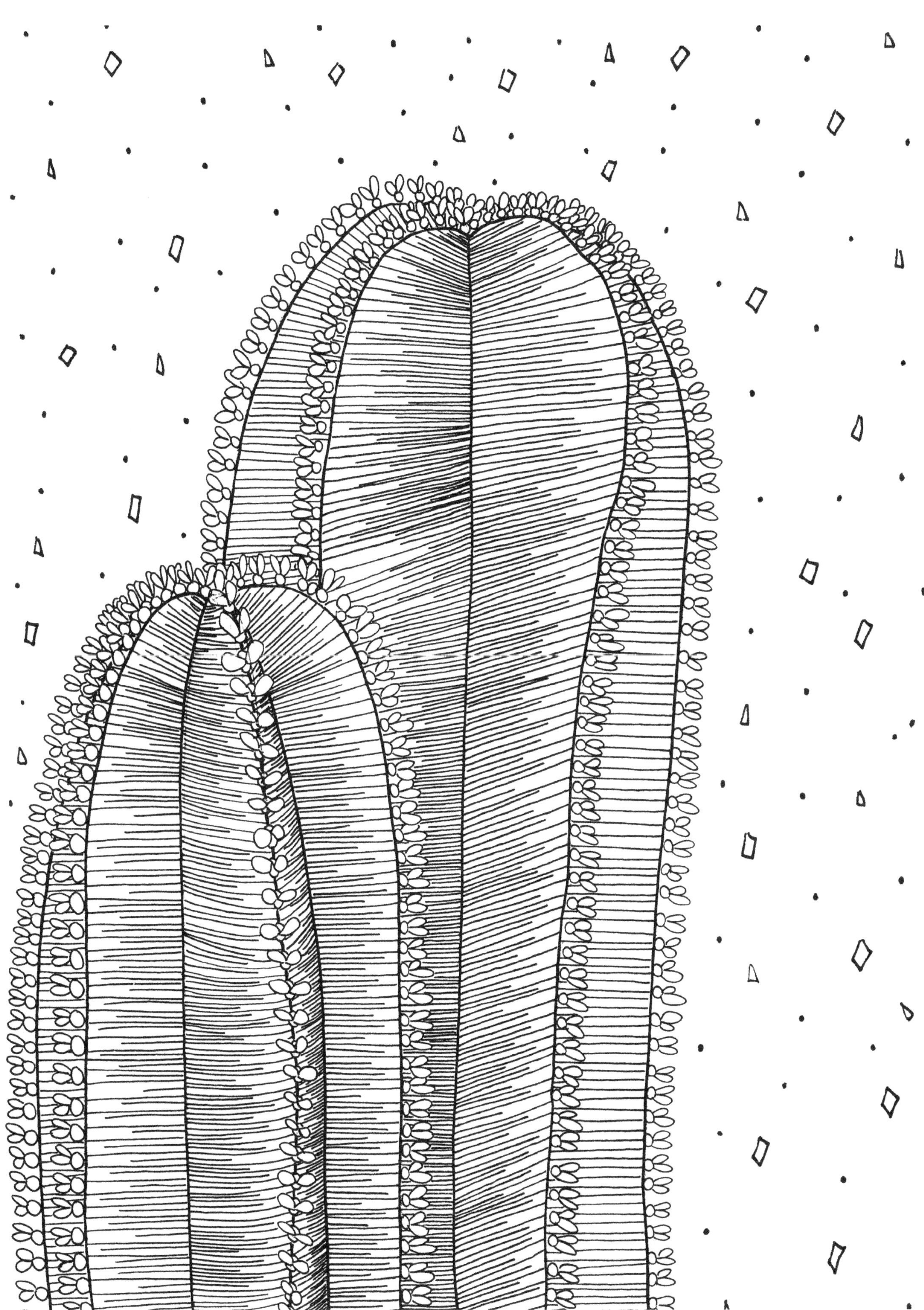

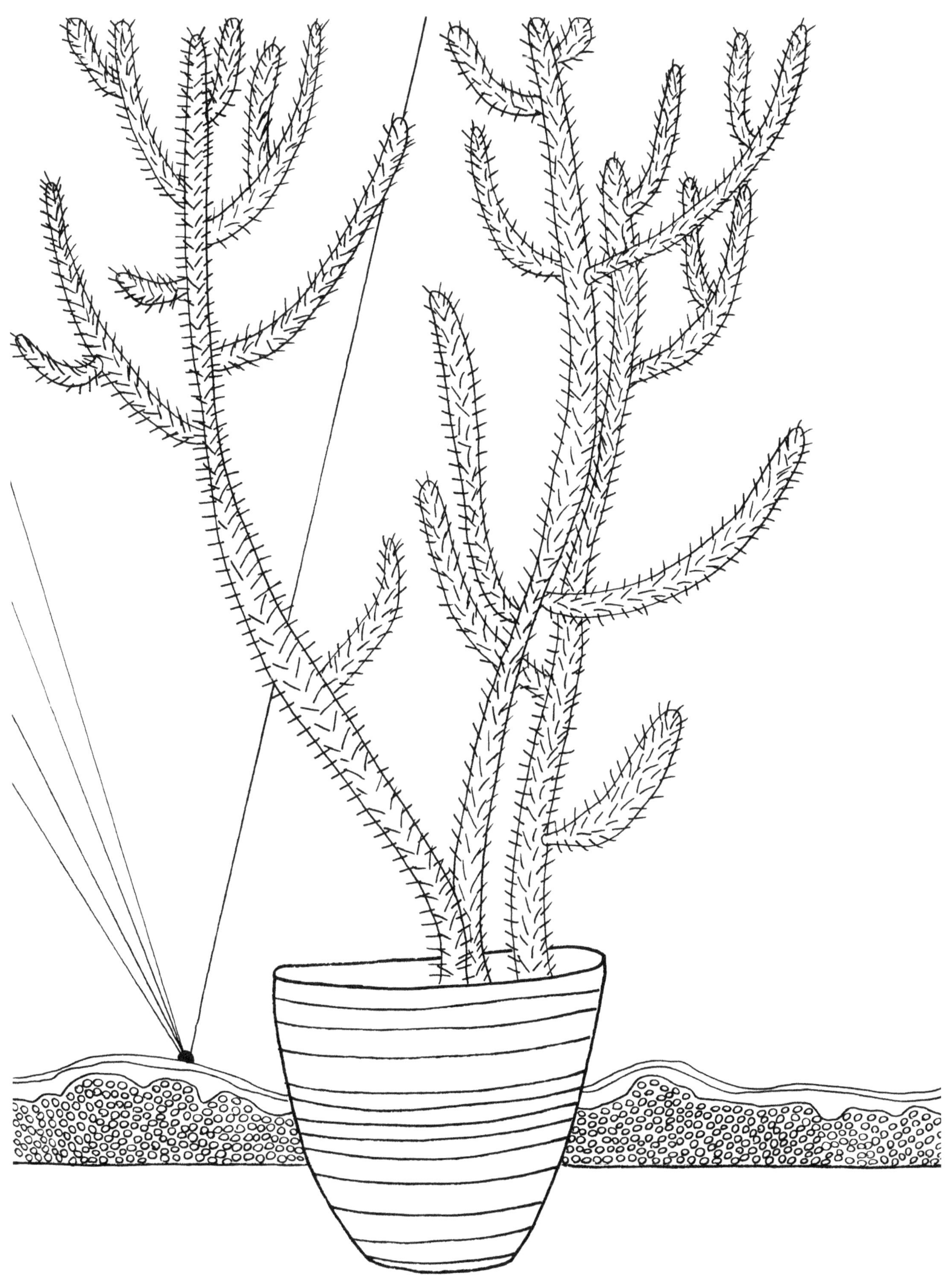

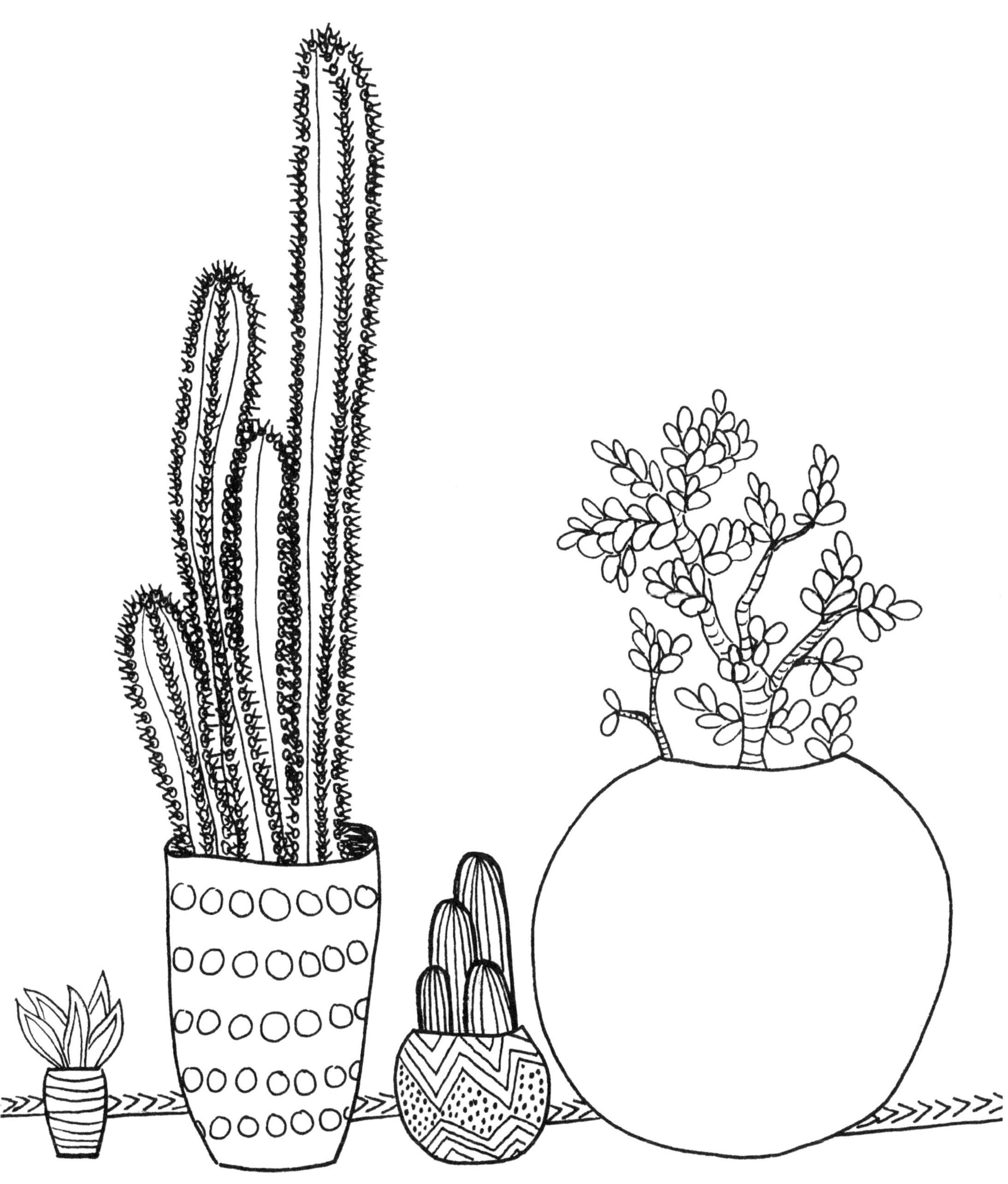

www.ingramcontent.com/pod-product-compliance
Lightning Source LLC
LaVergne TN
LVHW081254100826
845148LV00009B/1221

* 9 7 8 1 7 3 2 9 7 2 2 1 6 *